Grolier 9-96

A ROOKIE BIOGRAPHY

MARK TWAIN

Author of Tom Sawyer

By Carol Greene

CHILDRENS PRESS ®
CHICAGO

This book is for Sarah Bullock.

Samuel Langhorne Clemens (1835-1910)

Library of Congress Cataloging-in-Publication Data

Greene, Carol.
    Mark Twain : author of Tom Sawyer / Carol Greene.
        p.   cm. — (A Rookie biography)
    Summary: A simple biography of Samuel Clemens, who grew up on the
Mississippi River and gained literary renown under the name Mark
Twain.
    ISBN 0-516-04228-9
    1. Twain, Mark, 1835-1910—Biography—Juvenile literature.
2. Authors, American—19th century—Biography—Juvenile literature.
[1. Twain, Mark, 1835-1910. 2. Authors, American.] I. Title. II. Series:
Greene, Carol. Rookie biography.
PS1331.G76   1992
818'.409—dc20
[B]   91-40829
                                                                      CIP
                                                                      AC

Mark Twain
was a real person.
He lived from 1835 to 1910.
His real name was
Samuel Langhorne Clemens.
But he used Mark Twain
for his many books.
This is his story.

TABLE OF CONTENTS

Halley's comet (above) can be seen in the sky about once every 75 years. Below: The house at Florida, Missouri, where Samuel Clemens (Mark Twain) was born.

Chapter 1

River Boy

On November 30, 1835,
people looked up
at the night sky.
There glowed Halley's comet,
strange and wonderful.

That same night,
in the tiny town of
Florida, Missouri,
a little boy was born.
His parents named him
Samuel Langhorne Clemens.

Young Sam
wasn't strong.
Later, he said
he lived mostly
on cod-liver oil
and other
medicines his
mother gave him.

Mark Twain's mother

When Sam was almost four,
his family moved to
Hannibal, Missouri, a town
on the Mississippi River.
Sam's father opened
a general store.

When Sam was five,
he started school
in a little log house.
But the lessons he liked best
were not learned in school.

Mark Twain visiting his home in Hannibal, Missouri

Mark learned to tell stories from the
older black people in Hannibal.

He learned how to tell stories
from black people in town.
He learned about nature from the river.
He learned about life
from the people
who lived on the
mighty Mississippi River.

Every day, Sam heard the cry:
"Steamboat a-comin'!"
Down to the river he ran
with the other boys.
They all wanted to work
on a steamboat someday.

Steamboats carried people and freight
up and down the Mississippi River.

When Sam was eleven,
his father died.
Now the Clemens family
was very poor.

Sam got a job
delivering newspapers.
He learned about
printing them, too.

Mark Twain
at age
fifteen

Orion Clemens (left) had a printing office
on the third floor of the middle building shown here.

Soon his brother, Orion,
started his own newspaper.
Sam went to work for him.
He helped with the printing
and he wrote things.

By 1853, Sam was ready
to leave Hannibal.
He was seventeen years old
and ready for adventures.

Mark Twain in 1853

Chapter 2

River Man

Sam spent a few years
moving from city to city.
He earned money by
working for printers.

One day, he decided
he would like to go
to South America
and make a lot of money.
But first he needed money
to *get* to South America.

Mark Twain's office in Keokuk, Iowa,
was moved to a museum in New York City.

Sam was walking down
Main Street in Keokuk, Iowa,
when a piece of paper blew by.
It stuck in a wall
and Sam pulled it out.
It was a fifty-dollar bill.

Sam was on his way.

Mark Twain
at age
twenty-four

In April, 1857, he got on
a steamboat, the *Paul Jones.*
It was going to New Orleans.
Sam could sail to
South America from there.

But on the boat, Sam
got an old feeling again.
Wouldn't it be grand to learn
to pilot a steamboat?

He talked the captain
into teaching him.
By the time the boat reached
New Orleans, Sam had
forgotten about South America.

Tower Rock on the
Mississippi River
was one of the
landmarks the
river pilots used to
help them guide
the steamboats.

For two years, he went
up and down the Mississippi
from New Orleans to St. Louis
and back again.
He learned every inch
of the river.

It was hard work,
but Sam loved it.
In 1859, he got
his river pilot's license.

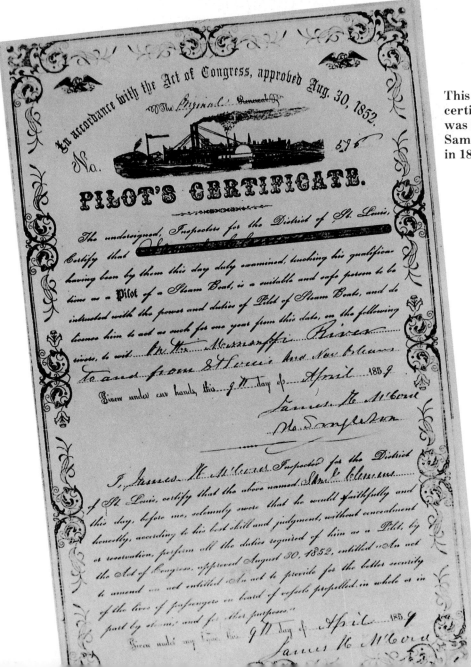

This pilot's certificate was issued to Samuel Clemens in 1859.

But Sam couldn't work
as a pilot for long.
In 1861, the Civil War began.

Sam fought for the South
for two weeks.
But he hated war.
So he and his brother, Orion,
went west to Nevada.

The Civil War lasted from 1861 to 1865.

Many men were going west
to get rich quickly.
Folks said the mountains
were full of silver and gold.

But Sam didn't
do much
digging for
riches. He spent
most of his time
watching other
people.

Virginia City, Nevada, during
the 1870s, when Mark Twain (inset) lived there

When he ran out of money,
Sam got a job
writing for a newspaper
in Virginia City, Nevada.

He wrote about the
Nevada government.
He also wrote funny things.
For the funny things, Sam
used a different name,
Mark Twain.

"Mark Twain" is river talk.
It means "two fathoms."
It means that the water
is twelve feet deep.
Boats can safely go through.

It was a perfect name for
a writer who loved the river.
Soon everybody
called Samuel Clemens
Mark Twain.

The cartoon at right
shows Mark Twain
riding the famous
Jumping Frog from
his story.
Cartoonists
loved to draw
funny pictures
of Mark Twain.

Chapter 3

Moving Around

Sam Clemens could never
stay in one place.
Neither could Mark Twain.
He left Nevada and went
to San Francisco to work
for another newspaper.

There he wrote a funny story,
"Jim Smiley and His Jumping Frog."
He sold it to a paper
in New York City.
Other papers printed it, too.
Many people liked that story.

Then Mark sailed to Hawaii
and wrote about life there.
When he got back, he spoke
to large groups of people
about his adventures.
He was a fine speaker.

Cartoon (left) shows Mark Twain speaking
about his trip to Hawaii (above).

Next, Mark moved to New York City. He wrote a book of funny stories. The frog story was in it.

This cartoon shows Mark Twain pulling stories from his imagination.

25

Mark said that book had
"a truly gorgeous gold frog"
on the cover.

Soon he was off to Europe.
He wrote another book,
The Innocents Abroad.

The steamship *Quaker City*, on which the "innocents" made their journey to Europe

On that trip,
Mark met Charles Langdon.
Charles showed him
a picture of his sister,
Olivia (Livy for short).

"From that day to this,"
Mark wrote much later,
"she has never been
out of my mind."

It took him a while
to ask Livy to marry him.
He was so busy
writing and speaking.

Olivia Langdon Clemens and Samuel Clemens about 1873

The first time he asked her,
Livy said no.
But she changed her mind,
and in 1870,
Mark and Livy were married.

Time to settle down
at last, thought Mark.

Chapter 4

Tom and Huck

Mark and Livy had
hard times at first.
Livy's father died.
Livy got very sick.
Their little boy died.

Mark was so upset that
he could hardly write.
But things got better.

Mark Twain's family (left to right), Susy, Jean, Olivia, and
Clara, lived in this big house in Hartford, Connecticut.

Mark Twain
with two
of his
daughters

The Twains had three girls:
Susy, Clara, and Jean.
The family lived in
Hartford, Connecticut.
Their house looked like
something from a fairy tale.

Mark stopped working for
newspapers and wrote books.
Roughing It told about
his adventures in the West.

Illustrations from the first edition of *The Adventures of Tom Sawyer*

Mark also had an idea
for another book,
a book about a boy
growing up in a town
on the Mississippi River.

The Adventures of Tom Sawyer
came out in 1876.
Many things in it are true.
They happened to Mark
or to his friends.

Mark called the town
in his book St. Petersburg.
But it is really Hannibal.
You can still see places there
where Tom had adventures.

As soon as *Tom Sawyer*
came out, Mark began
a book about Tom's friend.
Nine years later,
*The Adventures of
Huckleberry Finn* was ready.

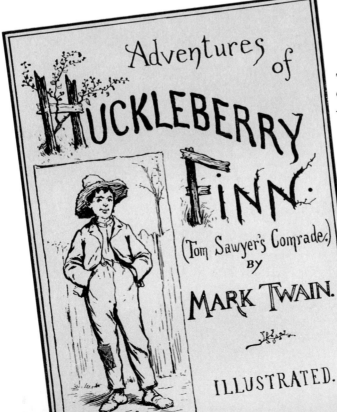

The first book
cover for
Huckleberry Finn

Illustrations of
Huck and Jim's
adventures on the
Mississippi River

Mark Twain
in the 1880s

In the book, Huck and
a runaway slave, Jim,
sail on a raft down
the Mississippi River.
Huck was a lot like a boy
Mark knew in Hannibal.

Many, many copies
of *Tom Sawyer* and
Huckleberry Finn have been sold.
Both children and grown-ups
still love these books today.

BJUYT KIOP M LKJHGFDSA:QWERTYUIOP;_-9BVBS4320W RT

HA

HARTFORD, DEC. 9.

DEAR BROTHER:

I AM TRYING T TO GET THE HANG OF THIS NEW F
FANGLED WRITING MACHINE, BUT·AM NOT MAKING
A SHINING SUCCESS OF IT. HOWEVER THIS IS THE
FIRST ATTEMPT I EVER HAVE MADE, & YET I PER-
CEIVETHAT I SHALL SOON & EASILY ACQUIRE A FINE
FACILITY IN ITS USE. I SAW THE THING IN BOS-
TON THE OTHER DAY & WAS GREATLY TAKEN WI:TH
IT. SUSIE HAS STRUCK THE KEYS ONCE OR TWICE,
& NO DOUBT HAS PRINTED SOME LETTERS WHICH DO
NOT BELONG WHERE SHE PUT THEM.
THE HAVING BEEN A COMPOSITOR IS LIKELY TO BE
A GREAT HELP TO ME, SINCE O NE CHIEFLY NEEDS
SWIFTNESS IN BANGING THE KEYS. THE MACHINE COSTS
125 DOLLARS. THE MACHINE HAS SEVERAL VIRTUES
I BELIEVE IT WILL PRINT FASTER TH
ONE MAY LEAN BACK IN HIS CHAIR &
PILES AN AWFUL STACK OF WORDS ON
IT DONT MUSS THINGS OR SCATTER I
OF COURSE IT SAVES PAPER.

                         SUSIE
NOW, & I FANCY I SHALL MAKE BETT
WORKING THIS TYPE-WRITER REMIND
ROBERT BUCHANAN, WHO, YOU REMEM
SET UP ARTICLES AT THE CASE WIT
LY PUTTING THEM IN THE FORM OF
WAS LOST IN ADMIRATION OF SUOH
INTELLECTUAL CAPACITY.

            YOUR·BROT

Mark Twain was one of the
first authors to use
a typewriter. He typed
this letter (above) to his brother.

THE TYPE-WRITER.

WHAT "MARK TWAIN" SAYS ABOUT IT.

Hartford, March 19, 1875.

GENTLEMEN: Please do not use my name in any
way. Please do not even divulge the fact that I
own a machine. I have entirely stopped using
the Type-Writer, for the reason that I never
could write a letter with it to anybody without
receiving a request by return mail that I would
not only describe the machine, but state what
progress I had made in the use of it, etc., etc.
I don't like to write letters, and so I don't want
people to know I own this curiosity-breeding
little joker. Yours truly,

SAML. L. CLEMENS.

Chapter 5

The Comet

Mark kept on traveling.
He made a lot of speeches
and a lot of money.
But he loved new inventions.
Often he lost money
trying to help the inventors.

He kept on writing, too.
Much of his writing
was funny. But Mark
could use funny
writing to say some
serious things.

Mark Twain cared about people who were not treated fairly.

Mark cared about poor people,
black people, and women.
He thought everyone should
be treated equally.
He said so again and again.

Mark, Livy, and Clara lived
in Europe for almost ten years.
Mark could earn more there
and pay back money he owed.
Jean and Susy stayed with
an aunt in Elmira, New York.

Mark Twain in
top hat (right),
around 1890,
and with a
group of friends
at his
seventieth birthday
party in New York.

Then, when Susy was 24,
she became ill and died.
That made Mark sad and angry.

In 1900, he and his family
moved to New York City.
People now thought Mark
was a very wise man.
They wanted to know
his ideas about everything.

Mark Twain
lived in this
house in
New York City.

Mark Twain with his daughter Clara (left) and in his home in Connecticut

In 1902, Livy became ill.
Mark took her to Italy,
because the weather there
was better for her.
But in 1904, she died.

Mark stayed busy then,
writing about his own life.
He worked on that book till 1908.
He used the money he made
to build a fine house, Stormfield,
near Redding, Connecticut.

**Twain at the window
of his writer's den
at Stormfield (below)**

But when Mark's daughter
Jean died too, he said,
"I shall never write anymore."
He didn't.

Four months later,
on April 21, 1910,
Mark Twain died
at the age of 74.

Mark Twain's grave
in Woodlawn Cemetery
at Elmira, New York

Once again, people looked
up at the night sky.
There glowed Halley's comet,
strange and wonderful.

Mark always felt
close to that comet.
He knew it would be there
the night he died
and he was glad.

Important Dates

1835	November 30—Born in Florida, Missouri, to Jane and John Marshall Clemens
1839	Family moved to Hannibal, Missouri
1859	Got river pilot's license
1861	Went to Nevada
1863	Began to use the name Mark Twain
1870	Married Olivia Langdon
1876	*The Adventures of Tom Sawyer* came out
1885	*The Adventures of Huckleberry Finn* came out
1891-1900	Lived mostly in Europe
1910	April 21—Died at Stormfield, near Redding, Connecticut

INDEX

Page numbers in boldface type indicate illustrations.

PHOTO CREDITS

AP/Wide World Photos—8, 14, 17, 18, 43

The Bettmann Archive—7, 19, 22 (2 photos), 24 (left), 25, 30 (bottom), 31, 35, 37, 39 (top). 40, 41 (right), 42 (top), 44, 45

Culver Pictures—2, 4 (top), 9, 15, 16, 28 (right), 32 (right), 34 (3 photos), 38, 39 (bottom), 41 (left)

Historical Pictures Service/Chicago—10, 12, 32 (left), 33, 36 (top)

North Wind Pictures Archives—4 (bottom), 6, 11 (2 photos), 20 (2 photos), 24 (right), 26, 30 (top), 36 (bottom)

UPI/Bettmann—28 (left), 42 (bottom)

Cover illustration by Steven Gaston Dobson

ABOUT THE AUTHOR

Carol Greene has degrees in English literature and musicology. She has worked in international exchange programs, as an editor, and as a teacher of writing. She now lives in Webster Groves, Missouri, and writes full-time. She has published more than 100 books, including those in the Childrens Press Rookie Biographies series.